Vegan Comfort Cooking

Delicious Vegan Comfort Food Recipes to Satisfy Every Craving

BY

Rachael Rayner

License Notes

Table of Contents

Introduction

I have been a vegan for just over ten years, and it was the best decision I have ever made. In 2008, I was diagnosed with type 2 diabetes; the doctors told me that there was no cure and I would be on insulin for the rest of my life. Initially, I accepted this, after all, doctors know everything, right? But during my first year of taking insulin and really not feeling too great from all the side effects, I decided to start researching alternative medicine and discovered that the biggest contributor to diabetes was a bad diet.

I had a terrible diet, I was overweight, I ate every greasy and unhealthy food you could think of and I didn't do any exercise. I started by doing simple things like replacing refined grains with whole grains and drinking water with my meals instead of soda. Then, I started adding more fruit and vegetables to my diet, and within a year, I had transitioned to veganism.

During this time, I would visit my doctor for my regular check-ups, he was impressed with my weight loss and the fact that he was able to reduce my insulin intake. Within two years of becoming vegan, I was diabetes free and I haven't looked back since.

However, despite the fact that I was cured from diabetes, lost loads of weight, and was healthier than I had ever been, there were a lot of meals that I really missed eating. I wasn't stupid enough to go and start buying buckets of fried chicken again, but I started researching the vegan versions of the foods I missed, and I was really impressed with what I found.

I was able to re-create all of my favorite comfort foods, but the healthy version and not feel in the least bit guilty about eating them, I was in heaven and so excited about my new discovery. I started holding dinner parties with my non-vegan friends and not tell them that what they were eating was vegan until the end of the meal, they were all fooled!

Not only are these meals finger-licking good, but they are also full of healthy nutritious ingredients that will boost your energy levels and make you feel fantastic. To begin, I would like to talk about some of the health benefits of veganism.

The Health Benefits of Veganism

You will often hear a lot of health experts advise that we need to eat animal products to get nutrients such as protein and calcium. When you think about this logically, it makes absolutely no sense because the animals that we get these products from are all vegetarians. Cows eat grass and hay; they get the calcium that they give us from the grass they eat. Calcium is a mineral found in soil that is absorbed by the grass. We actually get more calcium from dark leafy green vegetables than from drinking milk and eating cheese. When we consume dairy products, we lose 66% of the calcium through our urine. However, when we eat plant-based products containing calcium, the body absorbs 60 percent of it.

The same is true about protein; not only is it found in leafy green vegetables such as spinach, broccoli, asparagus, and alfalfa sprouts. There are also high levels of protein found in legumes such as white beans, lentils, pinto beans, split beans, black beans, navy beans, and kidney beans.

Efficient Kidney Functioning and Reduces Blood Sugar

I will start with this benefit because this is what helped to get rid of my type 2 diabetes. Several studies suggest that, in general, vegans have a high sensitivity to insulin, and they have lower blood sugar levels. Research has also found that the vegan diet is more effective than the diet recommended by the American Diabetes Association.

Protects Against Cancer

The World Health Organization suggests that approximately one-third of all cancers are preventable. One of the main factors for protecting the body against the disease is diet. For example, a diet that is high in legumes reduces the risk of colorectal cancer by between 9-18%.

Reduced Risk of Heart Disease

A diet high in fiber, legumes, fresh fruits, and vegetables reduces the risk of heart disease. A number of studies have found that vegans are up to 75% less likely to suffer from high blood pressure (a major contributing factor to heart disease) than non-vegans.

Vegan Foods to Eat

As you have read, a vegan diet means that you don't eat any animal products, and that includes dairy. If you are new to the vegan lifestyle, it can get a bit confusing about what foods to eat. So, to get you started, here is a comprehensive list of the foods you can and cannot eat on a vegan diet:

Vegetables: Broccoli, peppers, asparagus, kale, spinach, cauliflower, tomatoes.

Whole Grains: Couscous, kamut, spelt, buckwheat, amaranth, wild rice, brown rice, faro, barley, whole-wheat pasta, whole-wheat bread, quinoa, rolled oats.

Starchy Vegetables: Potatoes, sweet potatoes, squash.

Legumes: Lentils, peas, black beans, peanuts, chickpeas.

Healthy Fats: Coconut oil, olive oil, unsweetened coconut, avocados.

Fruits: Pears, berries, pineapples, apples, bananas, citrus fruits.

Seeds: Tahini, almonds, cashews, almond butter, pumpkin seeds, sunflower seeds, Macadamia nuts.

Spices and Seasonings: Black pepper, basil, sea salt, curry, turmeric, rosemary.

Drinks: Sparkling water, water, smoothies, fresh fruit and vegetable juices, unsweetened teas and coffees.

Plant-based Milk (unsweetened): Oat milk, cashew milk, coconut milk, almond milk.

Condiments: Nutritional yeast, salsa, lemon juice, vinegar, tamari, soy sauce, vegan mayonnaise, mustard.

Plant Based Proteins: Tofu and tempeh.

Foods Not to Eat on a Vegan Diet

Being on a vegan diet means you will need to read your food labels because there are some foods that contain animal products, but you don't know this until you read the ingredients, so I would strongly advise you to do this when you do your grocery shopping just to double-check.

Meat: Beef, lamb, pork, veal, organs, etc.

Poultry: Chicken, turkey, goose, duck, etc.

Eggs: Any type of egg.

Dairy: Yogurt, cheese, butter, ice cream etc.

Sea Food and Fish: Shrimp, mussles, crab, lobster, all fish, etc.

Bee Products: Royal Jelly, honey, etc.

A great way to start the vegan diet is making the healthier version of the foods you are used to eating, this book contains 30 of the most delicious comfort recipes for breakfast, lunch, dinner, and dessert.

Bon Appetite!

Breakfast Recipes

Peanut Butter Granola

Preparation Time: 35 Minutes/**Serves:** 2 Servings

What the better way to start the day than a combination of energizing peanut butter and crunchy granola?

Ingredients

- ¼ teaspoon of vanilla
- 2 tablespoons of pure maple syrup
- ¼ teaspoon of cinnamon
- 2 tablespoons of peanut butter
- 1 cup of oats
- Cooking spray
- Non-dairy milk

Directions

1. Prepare the oven by preheating it to 325 degrees F.

2. Coat a cookie sheet with cooking spray.

3. In a large microwaveable mixing bowl, combine the peanut butter and maple syrup and microwave in short intervals until the everything is melted together.

4. Remove the bowl from the microwave and stir to combine.

5. Add the cinnamon and vanilla to the peanut butter mixture and stir to combine.

6. Add the oats and stir to coat.

7. Spread the oat mixture onto the cookie sheet and bake for 10 minutes until slightly browned.

8. Once cooked, remove the granola from the oven and leave it to cool down until it becomes crunchy.

9. Serve with non-dairy milk.

Breakfast Tofu Tacos

Preparation Time: 45 Minutes/**Serves:** 8 Servings

This hearty combination of tacos and tofu will make you want to jump out of bed in the morning.

Ingredients

- ¼ cup of salsa
- 2 teaspoons of onion powder
- ½ teaspoon of garlic powder
- 2 tablespoons of bragg liquid aminos
- ¼ cup of nutritional yeast
- 1 package of drained extra firm tofu
- ¼ teaspoon of ground turmeric
- 8 warmed corn tortillas
- ¼ cup of whole-wheat flour
- Fresh cilantro for topping
- White onions for topping
- Greens of your choice for topping

Directions

1. After draining the tofu, place it onto a plate, cover with another plate and place a heavy metal weight over the top. Let it sit for a few minutes until all excess liquid has been drained from the tofu.

2. Crumble the tofu into a large bowl and add the garlic powder, turmeric, onion powder, flour and nutritional yeast. Toss to combine.

3. Add the liquid aminos and toss to combine.

4. heat a large frying pan over a medium temperature and cook the tofu mixture until crisp and brown.

5. Arrange the tortillas onto plates, spoon the tofu mixture onto them, top with salsa and toppings and serve.

Banana Bread

Preparation Time: 50 Minutes/**Serves:** 8 Servings

Single-handedly the best bread you've ever tasted!

Ingredients

- ½ teaspoon of salt
- 3 tablespoons of olive oil
- 1 cup of white flour
- 1 cup of wholemeal flour
- 2 teaspoons of baking powder
- 1 teaspoon of cinnamon
- 1 teaspoon of allspice
- ⅓ cup of brewed black coffee
- 3 tablespoons of chia seeds
- ½ cup of brown sugar
- 2 medium mashed bananas

Directions

1. Prepare the oven by preheating it to 350 degrees F.

2. Line a loaf pan with baking paper and put it to one side.

3. In a mixing bowl, combine the sugar and olive oil and whisk until it becomes fluffy.

4. Add 6 tablespoons of water to the chia seeds and stir to combine.

5. Add the chia seeds to the olive oil mixture and stir to combine.

6. Add the mashed bananas and coffee and stir to combine.

7. Sif the salt, raising agents, and flours and fold them into the wet mixture.

8. Pour the batter into the loaf pan and bake until the bread turns brown.

9. Remove the pan from the oven and serve warm.

Oatmeal Berry Waffles

Preparation Time: 55 Minutes/**Serves:** 6 Servings

This delicious combination of oatmeal and berries makes the perfect start to your day.

Ingredients

- ½ teaspoon of salt
- 2 tablespoons of canola oil
- 1 teaspoon of pure vanilla extract
- 3 tablespoons of pure maple syrup
- 1 ½ cups of unsweetened almond milk
- 1 tablespoon of baking powder
- ¼ teaspoon of ground allspice
- 1 cup of white whole-wheat flour
- ⅓ cup of unsweetened applesauce
- 1 ½ cups of frozen berries
- 1 cup of quick cooking oats

Directions

1. Sift the salt, allspice, baking powder and flour into a large mixing bowl.

2. Add the oats and stir to combine.

3. Create a hole in the middle and add the applesauce, maple syrup, milk, vanilla, blueberries and oil. Stir together thoroughly, put the batter to one side and leave it to sit for a few minutes to thicken.

4. Coat a waffle iron with oil and pour around half a cup of batter onto it.

5. Once cooked, remove and serve.

Delicious Upma

Preparation Time: 25 Minutes/**Serves:** 4 Servings

A mouth-watering Indian style breakfast bursting with flavors.

Ingredients

- ½ teaspoon of salt
- A small pinch of hing
- ½ cup of olive oil
- 1 small onion finely chopped
- 3 cups of water
- 1 teaspoon of black mustard seeds
- ¼ cup of chopped fresh cilantro leaves
- 1 small finely chopped green chili
- ½ teaspoon of turmeric
- 1 teaspoon of cumin seeds
- 5 curry leaves
- 1 cup of creamed wheat
- Coconut flakes for garnish
- Fresh cilantro leaves for garnish

Directions

1. Heat a heavy dry pan over a medium temperature and then roast the creamed wheat until it begins to brown. Stir frequently until to prevent it from burning.

2. Heat the oil in a large saucepan over a medium temperature and add the cumin and mustard seeds. Cook until the seeds begin to pop and then add the rest of the spices apart from the salt.

3. Add the cilantro, onion, and chili and stir to combine.

4. Add the salt, water and leave the ingredients to boil for a few minutes.

5. Add the roasted creamed wheat and leave it to boil for about two minutes while stirring.

6. Garnish with coconut flakes and cilantro leaves, divide onto plates and serve.

Fruit Salad

Preparation Time: 40 Minutes/**Serves:** 10 Servings

This combination of juicy and succulent fruits will kickstart your day.

Ingredients

- ½ cup of water
- 2 cups of grapes
- ¼ cup of chopped pecans
- 2 cups of sliced strawberries
- The juice of 1 lemon
- 1 box of sugar-free instant vanilla pudding mix
- 2 medium diced bananas
- 1 can of pineapple tidbits (drain the juice and keep)
- 2 diced medium apples

Directions

1. In a large bowl, combine the lemon juice and apples and toss together thoroughly.

2. Add the grapes, pecans, pineapple and strawberries.

3. In another bowl, combine the pineapple juice, the pudding mix and whisk together thoroughly.

4. Pour the pudding mixture on top of the fruits, put in the fridge for an hour to chill before serving.

Gravy and Biscuits

Preparation Time: 45 Minutes/**Serves:** 2 Servings

It doesn't get much better than Southern comfort foods! These biscuits and gravy are so satisfying.

Ingredients for the Biscuits

- ½ cup of cold vegan butter
- Vegan butter for brushing
- ½ teaspoon of baking soda
- 1 teaspoon of salt
- 1 tablespoon of baking powder
- 1 cup of unsweetened vegan milk
- 2 cups of all-purpose flour
- Flour for the work surface

Ingredients for the Gravy

- ¼ cup of dry red wine
- 2 tablespoons of vegan butter
- ¼ cup of flour
- 2 cups of vegetable broth
- ½ teaspoon of garlic powder
- 1 teaspoon of dry thyme
- ½ tablespoon of onion powder

Directions

1. Prepare the oven by preheating it to 450 degrees F.

2. Lay baking paper over a baking sheet and put it to one side.

3. In a large bowl, combine the dry ingredients for the biscuits.

4. Use a pastry cutter to cut in the cold vegan butter until the dough turns into a coarse meal. Do this quickly so that the butter doesn't melt.

5. Add the milk and work it into the dough.

6. Add some flour to your work surface, put the dough onto it and form 1-inch thick round flat balls.

7. Use a biscuit cutter to cut out the biscuits and arrange them onto the prepared baking sheet.

8. Brush the biscuits with butter and bake until they turn golden brown, this should take approximately 15 minutes.

9. Once cooked, turn the oven off and leave them there to keep warm.

10. While the biscuits are cooking prepare the gravy by combining the garlic powder, onion and one cup of vegetable broth in a saucepan.

11. Bring the broth to a boil and turn the heat down to medium.

12. Add the butter and flour and whisk together thoroughly until there are no lumps.

13. Leave the ingredients to thicken for about 10 minutes and then add the rest of the vegetable broth with the red wine and thyme. Cover and cook for on the lowest temperature for 15-20 minutes stirring every so often.

14. Once the gravy is ready, remove the biscuits from the oven, divide onto plates, pour the gravy over the top and serve.

Lunch Recipes

Cheddar Broccoli Soup

Preparation Time: 1 Hour 5 Minutes/**Serves:** 4 Servings

This America classic is packed full of rich creamy goodness, the perfect comfort food for a cozy night in by the fire.

Ingredients

- Olive oil
- Salt and pepper
- Hot sauce
- ¼ cup of nutritional yeast
- ¼ cup of cashews
- 1 cup of vegan milk
- 4 cups of broccoli florets
- 4 cups of vegetable broth
- 1 diced onion
- 3 cloves of minced garlic
- 2 medium carrots peeled and chopped
- 1 large potato peeled and diced
- French bread to serve

Directions

1. In a large saucepan, heat some olive oil and sauté the onions until they become translucent. This should take approximately 5 minutes.

2. Add the garlic and continue to sauté.

3. Add the remaining vegetables apart from the broccoli, the cashews and vegetable broth. Bring the ingredients to a boil and then turn down the heat to low and leave it to simmer for 20 minutes until the vegetables become tender.

4. Blend the soup with an immersion blender until it becomes smooth.

5. Add the broccoli, milk, hot sauce and nutritional yeast, bring it to a boil and then reduce the temperature and leave the soup to simmer for 10 minutes.

6. Spoon into bowls and serve with French bread.

Vegan Tuna Salad Sandwich

Preparation Time: 10 Minutes/**Serves:** 4 Servings

You will be surprised at what you can do with chickpeas, even your non-vegan friends will think they are eating tuna.

Ingredients

- Salt and pepper
- 8 slices of bread
- ¼ teaspoon of dry dill
- 1 tablespoon of maple syrup
- 1 tablespoon of mustard
- 2 tablespoons of tahini
- ½ cup of diced celery
- ½ cup of diced red onion
- 1 can of chickpeas rinsed and drained

Directions

1. Combine all the ingredients in a large bowl and use a fork to mash the chickpeas together.

2. Spoon onto bread and serve.

Simple Curry

Preparation Time: 45 Minutes/**Serves:** 4 Servings

Warm, creamy, and delicious, you can whip up a curry in a matter of minutes with these simple ingredients.

Ingredients

- Salt
- Water
- 1 tablespoon of minced ginger
- 1 clove of minced garlic
- 1 cup of cauliflower
- ¼ cup of curry powder
- 2 cans of chickpeas rinsed and drained
- 1 can of coconut milk
- 1 ½ cups of pumpkin peeled and cubed
- Naan bread

Preparation

1. Combine the coconut milk, curry powder, cauliflower and pumpkin in a saucepan and bring the ingredients to a boil. Lower the temperature and leave it to simmer. Keep checking the ingredients because you may need to add some water after as the pumpkin cooks.

2. Once the vegetables are tender, pour the curry into a food processor and blend until smooth.

3. Pour the curry back into the saucepan and add the chickpeas and heat through.

4. Spoon the curry onto plates and serve with naan bread.

Portobello Burgers

Preparation Time: 25 Minutes/**Serves:** 4 Servings

This delicious burger will give traditional red meat a run for its money.

Ingredients

- Salt and pepper
- ¼ cup of olive oil
- ½ teaspoon of garlic powder
- ½ teaspoon of onion powder
- 1 teaspoon of dried oregano
- 1 tablespoon of maple syrup
- 1 tablespoon of balsamic vinegar
- 1 avocado
- 1 sliced tomato
- 4 hamburger buns
- 4 portobello mushrooms de-stemmed

Directions

1. Combine the oregano, onion powder, garlic powder, balsamic vinegar, olive oil, salt and pepper and whisk to combine.

2. Marinate the mushrooms in the sauce for 15 minutes.

3. Grill the mushrooms for 5 minutes on each side.

4. Toast the hamburger buns

5. Arrange the mushrooms onto the buns, top with tomato and avocado and serve.

Loaded Nachos

Preparation Time: 30 Minutes/**Serves:** 6 Servings

Loaded with vegetables and healthy proteins, this lunch recipe is every vegans dream come true.

Ingredients

- 2 sliced avocados
- 1 tablespoon of vegetable oil
- 1 bag of tortilla chips
- 1 cup of salsa
- 1 diced red onion
- 1 sliced red pepper
- 1 can of black beans
- 2 cups of vegan cheese

Directions

1. Prepare the oven by preheating it to 350 degrees F.

2. In a large saucepan, heat the olive oil over a medium temperature, and sauté the onion and red pepper for 10 minutes.

3. Add the salsa and warm through.

4. Arrange the tortilla chips on a baking tray and top with the beans, veggies and cheese.

5. Bake for about 10 minutes until the cheese melts

6. Remove the tortilla chips from the oven, op with salsa and avocado and serve.

Browned Butter Pasta

Preparation Time: 25 Minutes/**Serves:** 4 Servings

This gourmet dish is creamy and delicious, you can whip it up in minutes and don't be surprised if you go for a second helping.

Ingredients

- ½ cup of vegan Parmesan
- 2 cloves of minced garlic
- ¼ cup of nutritional yeast
- ¼ cup of vegan butter
- 1 cup of pasta

Directions

1. Cook the pasta according to the directions on the packet. Drain the water and set it to one side.

2. Heat the butter in a saucepan over a medium temperature, add the garlic and sauté until it becomes fragrant.

3. Add the nutritional yeast, add the pasta and stir to combine.

4. Spoon onto plates, top with Parmesan cheese and serve.

Mushroom Creamy Soup

Preparation Time: 55 Minutes/**Serves:** 4 Servings

No matter what time of the year it is, this mushroom soup is warm, healing, and brilliantly satisfying.

Ingredients

- Salt and pepper
- ½ teaspoon of dry thyme
- 1 tablespoon of dry white wine
- 2 tablespoons of vegan butter
- ½ cup of cashews
- 3 cups of vegetable broth
- 1 cup of vegan milk
- 3 cloves of minced garlic
- 1 small diced onion
- 5 cups of fresh, chopped mushrooms
- French bread to serve

Directions

1. Heat the vegan butter in a saucepan over a medium temperature.

2. Sauté the garlic, mushrooms and onions for 10 minutes.

3. Add the seasoning, cashews, milk, wine, and the vegetable broth, bring the ingredients to a boil and then reduce the heat to low and leave the soup to simmer for 45 minutes.

4. Pour the soup into a food processor and blend until smooth.

5. Spoon the soup into bowls, season with salt and pepper and serve with French bread.

Dinner Recipes

Corn Casserole

Preparation Time: 50 Minutes/**Serves:** 6 Servings

This cruelty free version of corn casserole will send your taste buds into complete ecstasy.

Ingredients

- ½ cup of mushrooms
- ¼ cup of vegan butter
- 1 cup of unsweetened vegan milk
- 1-ounce box of vegan corn muffin mix
- 1 ounce can of cream style corn
- 2 cups of corn kernels

Directions

1. Prepare the oven by preheating it to 350 degrees F.

2. In a large bowl, combine all the ingredients and mix them together thoroughly. Transfer the mixture into an oven safe baking dish.

3. Bake until the top turns golden brown in color, this should take around 45 minutes.

4. Remove from the oven and serve.

Vegan Fried Chicken

Preparation Time: 20 Minutes/**Serves:** 6 Servings

If you've missed fried chicken since turning vegan, not to worry, this version is even better than the original!

Ingredients

- ⅓ cup of water
- 2 tablespoons of spicy brown mustard
- 1 teaspoon of salt
- 1 ½ tablespoons of baking powder
- ½ teaspoon of cumin
- 1 teaspoon of paprika
- 1 teaspoon of garlic powder
- 1 teaspoon of onion powder
- ¼ cup of nutritional yeast
- 1 ½ cups of flour
- 1 cup of oil
- 1 pound of vegan chicken (tofu or seitan)

Directions

1. Combine the dry ingredients together in a large bowl.

2. In another bowl, combine the water and mustard and whisk together thoroughly.

3. Add ⅓ cup of the dry ingredients to the mustard mixture and whisk together to form a batter.

4. Heat the oil in a large frying pan over medium temperature.

5. Dip your meat replacement into the wet mixture and then into the dry ingredients and then arrange them in the frying pan.

6. Fry until golden brown.

7. Remove from the frying pan and serve with dipping sauces or on a bun for a chicken sandwich.

Vegan Pot Pie

Preparation Time: 20 Minutes/**Serves:** 4 Servings

There is nothing more comforting than a pot pie on a cold winter night. You can't go wrong with this delicious and hearty recipe.

Ingredients

- Salt and pepper
- 1 tablespoon of olive oil
- 2 bay leaves
- ¾ teaspoons of thyme
- ½ teaspoon of sage
- ¼ cup of flour
- ½ cup of unsweetened vegan milk
- ½ cup of fresh corn
- 2 large diced potatoes
- 2 finely chopped stalks of celery
- 2 cups of vegetable broth
- 2 cloves of minced garlic
- 1 diced onion
- 1 roll of vegan biscuits

Directions

1. Prepare the oven by preheating it to 425 degrees F.

2. Heat the olive oil over medium temperature and sauté the garlic and onions for 5 minutes.

3. Add the vegetable broth, the milk, and slowly add the flour.

4. Whisk the ingredients together thoroughly.

5. Add the rest of the ingredients apart from the biscuits and let the mixture simmer until it has thickened into a gravy. This should take about 15 minutes. Remove the bay leaves.

6. Transfer the ingredients into an oven proof dish and arrange the biscuits over the top.

7. Bake until the biscuits turn golden brown in color, this should take around 15 minutes.

8. Once cooked, remove from the oven and serve.

Macaroni and Cheese

Preparation Time: 20 Minutes/**Serves:** 4 Servings

This vegan style macaroni and cheese is way up there on the list of ultimate comfort foods. Bursting with a variety of flavors, this dish will have you coming back for seconds.

Ingredients

- Salt
- Half cup of vegan Parmesan cheese
- ¼ teaspoon of chipotle powder
- ½ teaspoon of chili powder
- ½ teaspoon of garlic powder
- ¼ cup of nutritional yeast
- 1 cup of soaked cashews
- 1 cup of dry pasta

Directions

1. Cook the pasta according to the directions on the package.

2. Combine the cashews, nutritional yeast and seasoning and blend until creamy.

3. Combine the cheesy mixture with the cooked pasta, top with vegan Parmesan cheese, divide onto plates and serve.

Vegan Shephard's Pie

Preparation Time: 50 Minutes/**Serves:** 6 Servings

There are some things that you just can't live without and a traditional shepherd's pie is one of them!

Ingredients

- Salt
- 1 cup of vegan cheddar shreds
- ¼ cup of vegan butter
- ½ cup of non-dairy milk
- 3 potatoes
- 2 cloves of minced garlic
- 1 teaspoon of thyme
- 1 cup of vegetable broth
- ½ cup of red wine
- 1 cup of cauliflower florets
- 1 carrot peeled and diced
- 1 diced onion
- 1 cup of dry green lentils

Directions

1. Prepare the oven by preheating it to 425 degrees F.

2. Boil the potatoes for 30 minutes. Drain the water and leave them to cool down completely before removing the skins.

3. Add the butter and milk and mash to desired consistency and set to one side.

4. Heat the oil in a frying pan and sauté the garlic and onions until they become tender.

5. Add the lentils, thyme, wine, and broth and bring the ingredients to a boil.

6. Reduce the temperature to low and leave the ingredients to simmer for 30 minutes.

7. Add the vegetables and cook for a further 10 minutes until the lentils become tender.

8. Transfer the ingredients into an oven proof dish, cover with the mashed potatoes and vegan cheese and bake for 15 minutes until the mashed potatoes turn golden brown in color.

9. Once cooked, remove from the oven and serve.

Spaghetti and Meatballs

Preparation Time: 35 Minutes/**Serves:** 4 Servings

Who doesn't love spaghetti and meatballs? This recipe is so close to the real thing that you will fool even your non-vegan friends.

Ingredients

- 1 teaspoon of dry basil
- ½ teaspoon of garlic powder
- 2 flax eggs
- 1 cup of breadcrumbs
- 1 can of chickpeas rinsed and drained
- 1 roasted eggplant
- 2 tablespoons of tomato paste
- 2 cups of spaghetti sauce
- 8 ounces of dry spaghetti

Directions

1. Prepare the oven by preheating it to 375 degrees F.

2. Cook the pasta according to the directions on the packet, drain the water and set it to one side.

3. In a food processor combine the chickpeas, eggplant, tomato paste and seasoning pulse slightly so that the mixture is still chunky.

4. Pour the mixture into a bowl, add the flax eggs and the breadcrumbs and stir to combine.

5. Use your hands to roll the mixture into balls and arrange them onto a baking sheet.

6. Bake for 30 minutes until the balls are browned.

7. Arrange the pasta onto plates, top with spaghetti sauce and meatballs.

Scalloped Potatoes

Preparation Time: 1 Hour 35 Minutes/**Serves:** 4 Servings

There is nothing better than creamy, cheesy potatoes on a cold winter night.

Ingredients

- Salt and pepper
- ¼ cup of flour
- ¼ cup of vegan butter
- 2 cups of unsweetened vegan milk
- 4 large potatoes, peeled and sliced

Directions

1. Prepare the oven by preheating it to 350 degrees F.

2. Melt the butter in a saucepan over a medium temperature.

3. Slowly add the flour while whisking.

4. Add the milk, salt and pepper and continue to whisk until the mixture has turned into a thick sauce.

5. Arrange the potatoes in an oven proof dish.

6. Pour the sauce over the top and stir to combine.

7. Cover with foil and bake for 30 minutes.

8. Remove the foil and bake for another 60 minutes until the top has become tender and browned.

9. Once cooked, remove from the oven, divide onto plates and serve.

Dessert Recipes

Nice Cream Mint Chocolate Chip

Preparation Time: 10 Minutes/**Serves:** 2 Servings

There are plenty of ways you can eat ice-cream, and this is one of them just a healthier and more delicious version.

Ingredients

- A handful of carob chips
- Vanilla nut milk
- ¼ teaspoon of mint extract
- 2 ripe frozen, sliced bananas

Directions

1. Combine the banana and the mint extract into the food processor and blend on high.

2. Slowly add the nut milk until you get your desired consistency.

3. Add the carob chips and serve.

Nice Cream with Chocolate S'Mores

Preparation Time: 10 Minutes/**Serves:** 4 Servings

Unless someone tells you, you will never know that this dessert is vegan. It's packed full of sweet gooey irresistible goodness!

Ingredients

- Non-dairy milk
- 4 vegan graham crackers
- Vegan marshmallows
- ¼ cup of vegan marshmallow fluff
- ¼ cup of cocoa powder
- 2 frozen, sliced bananas

Directions

1. Combine the cocoa powder and the bananas in a food processor and blend to combine.

2. Slowly pour in the milk until your desired consistency has been reached.

3. Pour the mixture into a bowl and top with the vegan marshmallow fluff, then crumble the graham crackers over the top and the marshmallows.

4. Serve cold.

Fancy Fudge

Preparation Time: 30 Minutes/**Serves:** 24 Servings

This creamy delicious fudge tastes exactly like the real thing, but a healthier version. You can eat as much as you like without feeling guilty.

Ingredients

- 1 cup of peanut butter
- ½ cup of vegan butter
- 3 tablespoons of maple syrup
- 1 teaspoon of vanilla extract
- Salt
- A pinch of cinnamon

Directions

1. Combine all the ingredients together in a food processor and blend until smooth.

2. Pour into a freezer safe dish and freeze for 20 minutes before serving.

Chocolate Dirt Cups

Preparation Time: 1Hour 10 Minutes/**Serves:** 4 Servings

Tasty, chewy, chocolate delight. You will have a field day with this one.

Ingredients

- 1 bag of vegan gummy worms
- 8 crushed Oreo cookies
- 1 teaspoon of vanilla extract
- ¼ cup of non-dairy milk
- ½ cup of maple syrup
- ½ cup of raw cocoa powder
- 2 avocados

Directions

1. Combine the sweetener, vanilla, avocados and cocoa into a food processor and blend until smooth.

2. Slowly add the milk and continue blending.

3. Pour the mixture into a bowl and put it in the fridge for 60 minutes.

4. Line the bottom of 4 cups with crushed Oreos and gummy worms.

5. Pour the chilled pudding into the cups and top with more crushed Oreos and gummy worms.

Brownie Beanie Blackies

Preparation Time: 30 Minutes/**Serves:** 9 Servings

Healthy mouth-watering brownies packed with succulent ingredients that the whole family can enjoy.

Ingredients

- 1 teaspoon of baking soda
- 2 teaspoons of vanilla extract
- ¼ cup of vegan butter
- ½ cup of maple syrup
- ½ cup of cocoa powder
- 2 flax eggs
- ½ cup of oat flour
- 1 cup of non-dairy milk
- 1 can of sodium free black beans drained and rinsed

Directions

1. Prepare the oven by preheating it t0 350 degrees F.

1. Combine all the ingredients apart from the milk into a food processor and blend until smooth.

2. Slowly add the milk and continue to blend.

3. Pour the mixture into a baking pan and bake for 20 minutes.

4. Once cooked, remove the brownies from the oven, slice and serve.

Simple Chocolate Chip Cookies

Preparation Time: 25 Minutes/**Serves:** 12 Servings

Everyone loves chocolate chip cookies, but with this healthier version, you will love them even more.

Ingredients

- 1 flax egg
- ½ teaspoon of salt
- ½ cup of vegan butter
- 1 teaspoon of baking powder
- 1 teaspoon of vanilla extract
- 1 cup of unpacked brown sugar
- 1 cup of carob chips
- 1 cup of flour

Directions

1. Prepare the oven by preheating it to 350 degrees F.

2. Lay a baking tray with a parchment paper and set it to one side.

3. Combine all the ingredients in a large mixing bowl until they become thick and creamy.

4. Flour a work surface and roll the dough out.

5. Use a cookie cutter to cut out 12 cookies.

6. Arrange the cookies on the baking tray and bake for 15 minutes until they become golden brown in color.

7. Once cooked, remove the cookies from the oven and serve hot.

Monkey Bread

Preparation Time: 45 Minutes/**Serves:** 10 Servings

You will never taste a bread so sweet and delicious as this one.

Ingredients

- ¼ cup of cranberries
- 1 tablespoon of cinnamon
- ½ cup of unpacked brown sugar
- ½ cup of melted vegan butter
- 1 roll of vegan biscuits torn into pieces

Preparation

1. Prepare the oven by preheating it to 350 degrees F.

2. Line a baking tray with parchment paper and set it to one side.

3. Combine the cinnamon and brown sugar in a large mixing bowl.

4. Melt the butter in a separate bowl.

5. Take the torn biscuit pieces and dip them into the butter and then into the sugar mixture.

6. Arrange the biscuit pieces onto the baking tray and top with the cranberries.

7. Pour the rest of the butter over the top of the biscuit pieces and bake for 30 minutes.

8. Once cooked, remove from the oven and serve hot.

Lemon Tarts

Preparation Time: 2 Hours 20 Minutes/**Serves:** 3 Servings

These no-bake, gluten free lemon tarts will brighten up your day with the first bite.

Ingredients for the Crust

- 1 teaspoon of lemon zest
- 2 tablespoons of lemon juice
- 2 tablespoons of maple syrup
- 2 tablespoons of melted coconut oil
- ¾ cup raw cashews
- 1 cup of shredded coconut

Ingredients for the Filling

- ¼ teaspoon of sea salt
- 1 teaspoon of vanilla extract
- 1 tablespoon of lemon zest
- ¼ cup of maple syrup
- ¼ cup of canned coconut milk
- ⅓ cup of coconut oil
- ½ a cup of lemon juice
- 1 cup of raw cashews soaked overnight

Directions

1. Grease a baking pan with some coconut oil.

2. To make the crust, combine the cashews and the shredded coconut in a food processor and pulse until the cashews are broken up into small pieces.

3. Add the lemon zest, lemon juice, maple syrup, and coconut oil and blend until fully combined.

4. Transfer the crust into the baking pan and press it along the bottom and the sides of the pan.

5. To make the filling, combine all the ingredients in the food processor and blend until smooth.

6. Pour the filling over the crust and put the baking tray in the fridge for 2 hours.

7. Once set, remove from the fridge and slice and serve.

Caramel Peanut Butter Rice Krispies

Preparation Time: 45 Minutes/**Serves:** 9 Servings

A tasty, crunchy sweet dessert that you are going to want to eat for breakfast, lunch, and dinner.

Ingredients for the Rice Krispies

- 6 cups of rice crisp cereal
- 1 teaspoon of vanilla extract
- ⅓ cup of creamy peanut butter
- ¼ cup of maple syrup
- ¾ cup of brown rice syrup

Ingredients for the Peanut Butter Drizzle

- 1-2 teaspoons of water
- 1 teaspoon of maple syrup
- 2 tablespoons of creamy peanut butter

Directions

1. Line a baking tray with parchment paper.

2. Combine the maple syrup and the brown rice syrup in a large saucepan and heat over a medium temperature. Let the ingredients come to a rolling boil for 1 minute and keep stirring so that it doesn't burn.

3. Remove the saucepan from the cooker and stir in the vanilla and the peanut butter until smooth.

4. Add the rice crisp cereal and stir to combine.

5. Scoop the mixture out into the baking pan and freeze for 10 minutes.

6. To make the peanut butter drizzle, combine the maple syrup and the peanut butter in a microwaveable bowl and heat in 30 second intervals until melted.

7. Remove the bowl from the microwave, add a teaspoon of water and whisk until smooth, if the mixture is too thick, add another teaspoon of water.

8. Take the krispies from the freezer, drizzle the peanut butter mixture over the top, and put the krispies back in the freezer for another 10 minutes.

9. Once set, remove from the freezer, slice into bars and serve.

Conclusion

I hope you have been able to enjoy some of the vegan comfort food recipes in this book. Whether you are new to veganism or you have been a vegan for a while, there is a wide range of meals for you to enjoy.

There is no need to stick to the recipes as they are; you can get creative with them and add or take away from some of the ingredients to suit your taste. If you are new to the vegan lifestyle, this cookbook will kickstart your diet, and if you are consistent and stick to healthy vegan recipes, you will begin to experience some of the benefits mentioned in the introduction.

If you have enjoyed this book, would you be so kind as to leave a review, not only will it help me but also help those who are interested in the book make an intelligent buying decision.

I wish you all the luck and success in the world!

Author's Afterthoughts

THANK YOU

Thanks ever so much to each of my cherished readers for investing the time to read this book!

I know you could have picked from many other books, but you chose this one. So, a big thanks for downloading this book and reading all the way to the end.

If you enjoyed this book or received value from it, I'd like to ask you for a favor. Please take a few minutes to post an honest and heartfelt review on Amazon.com. Your support does make a difference and helps to benefit other people.

Thanks for your Reviews!

Rachael Rayner

[illegible]

I know you could have picked from many other books but you chose this one. So a big thanks for downloading this book and reading all the way to the end.

If you enjoyed this book or received value from it, I'd like to ask you for a favor. Please take a few minutes to post an honest review [illegible]

[illegible]

Milton Keynes UK
Ingram Content Group UK Ltd.
UKHW051522300424
441994UK00044B/1486

9 798665 865836